Karol from Poland

Karol *from* Poland

The Life of Pope John Paul II for Children

Written by
M. L. Wilson, FSP
Ill. by C. Koch

Pauline
BOOKS & MEDIA
BOSTON

Library of Congress Cataloging-in-Publication Data

Wilson, M. Leonora.
    Karol from Poland : the life of Pope John Paul II for children / by M. Leonora Wilson ; illustrated by Carla Koch.
       p. cm.
    Summary: Traces the life of Karol Wojtyla from his childhood and student years in Poland through his ordination as a priest and election as Pope John Paul II, a missionary to the world.
    ISBN 0-8198-4205-2 (pbk.)
     1. John Paul II, Pope, 1920– Juvenile literature. 2. Popes—Biography—Juvenile literature. [1. John Paul II, Pope, 1920– 2. Popes.]

BX1378.5. W556 1999
282'.092—dc21
[B]
                                                        99-055302

Printed and published in the U.S.A.
by Pauline Books & Media, 50 Saint Pauls Avenue, Boston, MA 02130-3491.

www.pauline.org

Pauline Books & Media is the publishing house
of the Daughters of St. Paul, an international congregation of women religious
serving the Church with the communications media.

2 3 4 5 6 7   07 06 05 04 03 02

Contents

Karol's House

This is the story of a boy who grew up to do special things for God and other people. The boy's name is Karol Wojtyla. In English, "Karol" means "Charles." We say Karol's last name like this: VOY-TEE-WAH.

The house where Karol lived is very far away from yours. You can't walk there. You can't even drive there by car. Do you know why? It's because there is an ocean between you and it! You would have to take a jet to get to Karol's house.

The house where Karol used to live is in the small town of Wadowice. We say that name like this: VAH-DOE-VEE-CHAY. Wadowice is in the country of Poland.

If you ever go to Wadowice, follow the road until you reach Church Street. Then turn. Karol's house was #7. He lived on the second floor.

This house looks like most of the other houses on the street, but to Karol it was special. It was *his* house. It was the house of his mother, his father, and his brother, Edmund. It was a house he loved.

When Karol was born, on May 18, 1920, his family lived in another house. Then they moved. Karol was too small to remember the other house.

Mother, Father and Edmund

Karol's father was a soldier. Karol was very proud of him. He liked his father's uniform with its bright, brass buttons. He liked the shiny stars on the collar. But most of all he liked the special medal his father had won for being a good soldier. Karol thought that maybe he would be a soldier, too, someday.

Karol had a brother named Edmund. Edmund was twelve years older than Karol. When Edmund was at school and his father was at work, Karol would stay at home with his mother.

Mrs. Wojtyla cleaned the house. She sewed the clothes. She cooked many good things for her family to eat. Then, Mrs. Wojtyla would sit on one of the big chairs. She would put Karol on her lap and read him stories. Karol liked these stories. Some of the stories were about God.

Karol's mother told him that God loves us so much that he made us. She taught him that God's son Jesus loves us so much that he came to earth and died to save us from our sins.

Mrs. Wojtyla taught Karol that God is everywhere. She explained that God is always with us and never stops loving us. She told Karol that God wants to be our best friend. God wants us to talk to him. We talk to God when we pray. Karol's mother taught him how to pray. Karol began to pray every morning and every night. He liked talking to God!

The Market

Sometimes Karol would go with his mother to the market in the middle of the town. The market was like a big, outdoor store. You could buy all kinds of things there—food, clothes, candy and even animals! Going to the market was fun!

On the way to the market, Karol and his mother would talk. Sometimes they would talk about heaven. Sometimes they would talk about Mary, God's mother. Karol wanted to know more about Mary. He learned to love Mary very much.

"Mary will help you to be good," said Karol's mother. "She will teach you to be like Jesus. Then one day she will bring you to heaven."

"When can I go to heaven?" Karol asked.

"Not right now," his mother answered with a smile. "You can go to heaven when you die. Then you will see God our Father, Jesus, Mary and all the saints."

Karol thought about this. He said, "I guess I can wait a little while before going to heaven. I like being here with Mom and Dad and Edmund."

Inside God's House

On the way to the market one day, Karol and his mother stopped at their parish church. Karol had gone there many times with his father, too.

The church was very big, especially when Karol stood next to it. Its top went right up into the sky!

Over the doorway was a beautiful statue of God's mother, Mary. On the very top of the church was a cross. Karol knew that the church is a special place because it's God's own house.

Karol's mother took him inside. They walked slowly up to the front.

"Do you see that golden box?" Karol's mom whispered.

Karol looked. He saw a golden box that looked like a little house. Next to it was a special candle.

"That is Jesus' house," Karol's mother explained. "It's called a *tabernacle*. Jesus stays there day and night."

After that, Karol kept thinking of how special the church was. He hoped his mother would bring him back very often.

Karol's Friends

Karol liked to play outside with his friends. He had a lot of friends. They called him by a special nickname—"Lolek." We say this name like this: LOW-LECK.

Karol liked sports, especially running very fast and playing soccer. Karol liked to laugh with his friends. He liked to sing, too!

Karol was growing fast. Soon he was seven years old. It was time to go to school.

Karol was excited. The school he went to was a military school. It was only for boys. All the students wore special suits called uniforms. Karol was proud of his uniform. It reminded him of his father's army uniform. Now he looked more like his father. He felt very grown-up.

Karol got good grades in school. He liked to learn. He always tried to do his homework. He made many more new friends, too.

A Sad Good-bye

One day Karol's mother didn't feel well. She had to go to the hospital. It was not long before Karol's ninth birthday. Karol was sad. Edmund was sad. The brothers knew that their father was worried.

"Mother will come home soon," their father said softly.

But Karol's mother did not come home. God took her to heaven instead.

Karol cried. He missed his mother very much. He felt so lonely.

But then, Karol began to think. He thought of what his mother had told him about heaven. She had said that everyone in heaven is alive and happy. She had told him that the people in heaven care about the people on earth.

Karol said to himself, *My mother can still see me. My mother can still hear me. I can talk to her! She loves me. I'm still her boy.*

Karol knew that someday he would be with his mother again. Jesus had promised this. This made him feel much better.

More Changes

Soon Karol was eleven. He finished military school. Now it was time to go to another school.

At the new school, Karol learned more about math. He learned more about writing. He learned more about science. He even learned new languages.

Sometimes Karol and his friends put on plays. Sometimes they played soccer, or went hiking. Sometimes they went fishing or swimming. In the winter they went skiing together. Karol liked his new school. He studied hard. He played hard. He had many friends.

Karol was only at the new school one year when his brother Edmund became very sick. Edmund did not get better. He died and went to be with God in heaven. How much Karol missed his big brother!

Karol's father was sad again, too. But he said, "God wants Edmund in heaven. God loves Edmund. He knows what is best. We will trust God."

The Future...

Karol finished high school. He still didn't know what he would be. He didn't want to be a soldier anymore. Maybe he would be an actor! Maybe he would be a priest! He wasn't sure.

Karol thought and thought. He went to the big church to pray. He asked God to help him. In the church there was a beautiful statue. It was a statue of the Sacred Heart of Jesus. Karol knew the statue was not Jesus, but it reminded him of Jesus. It made him feel close to Jesus, the way his mother's picture made Karol feel close to her.

"Jesus, tell me what I should do," Karol prayed. "Should I be an actor? Should I be a priest? Should I be a miner? Whatever I will be, I ask you and your mother Mary to help me to be strong and good."

In 1938 Karol and his father moved to a bigger city called Krakow (CRACK-OW). There Karol went to school at the university.

While Karol and his father were in Krakow, something *terrible* happened. A war broke out in Poland. People were fighting and hurting each other. There was shooting. There was bombing. Tanks and soldiers were everywhere. Many people were killed. Others were put in prison. No one in Poland was free anymore. It was very sad.

Brave Karol

Karol couldn't go to school during the war, because all the schools were closed. So he went to work. First he worked as a miner. Later he worked in a factory. Karol studied every night after work. He also got together with his friends. Karol still thought he might be an actor someday. Sometimes he and his friends put on plays. But nobody could come to watch them. The soldiers who had taken over Poland would not let the people watch Polish plays. They wouldn't let them sing Polish songs.

One of Karol's best friends was named Jan. Jan was a tailor. Karol and Jan talked. They prayed together. They worried about Poland. Karol was brave. He wanted his country to be free again. Sometimes he tricked the soldiers. He brought secret messages right past them! Sometimes he even helped people escape from the soldiers. He saved them from being killed.

During this time, Karol's father became very, very sick. Soon God called him to heaven, too. First his mother, then his big brother, and now his father had died. Karol was all alone.

"Please help me," Karol asked Jesus and Mary. "I have no one else but you." He prayed and prayed.

What did God want Karol to do? Finally he knew. God wanted him to be a priest! He would have to study hard. Every day after work he went home and studied and studied!

A Dangerous Trip

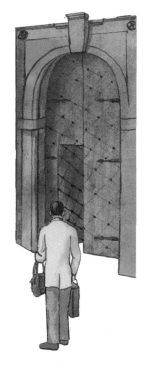

The war was growing worse. One Sunday, Karol heard a big noise outside his home. There was screaming. There was shooting. Karol listened. He knew what was happening. The soldiers were coming! They were taking all the men and boys to prison! If they put him in prison, he would never be able to become a priest!

Karol began to pray. He asked God to help him become a priest. He prayed for a very long time. The soldiers didn't come to his house. After a while, it was quiet again outside.

Early the next morning, a lady came. She was a guide. Karol followed her. They walked very quietly. They walked very quickly. It was a dangerous trip. Karol would never go back to his house again. He would never work in the factory again. He was going to another house, where the Archbishop of Krakow lived.

The lady and Karol walked and walked all through the town. They passed many enemy guards. Karol kept on praying. No one stopped them. The soldiers let them go by without asking even one question! Finally they were inside the archbishop's house. They were safe!

Karol thanked God. He thanked the lady. Now he could get ready to become a priest.

No one knew where Karol was. He didn't go to work at the factory. He wasn't at home. The soldiers were very, very angry! They wanted to find Karol, but they couldn't.

Father Karol

In 1945, the war finally ended. The soldiers left Poland. The schools opened up again. The people began to fix the streets and their houses.

Karol finished studying at the archbishop's house. Then he was ordained a priest. Now he was called Father Karol.

Father Karol celebrated his first Mass in the town where he was born. Many people came to the Mass. They were his friends. He thought about his father, his mother and Edmund. They were in heaven. He knew that they were happy for him. Father Karol was happy, too.

But soon there was trouble again! This time the Communists came to Poland. They tried to force the people to close all the churches. They told the people that there is no God. But the people knew better. They didn't believe the soldiers. Brave people opened the churches. They were not afraid.

Father Karol worked hard. He wanted to teach all the people about God. He especially wanted to teach all the children. The children loved Father Karol and he loved them. "They are my favorites," he said.

Father Karol played soccer with the children. He went swimming and hiking with them. He never missed a chance to teach them about God.

Messages

One day Father Karol went for a canoe ride with some boys and girls. While he was gone, someone came to look for him. The man carried an important message from the cardinal.

The note was brought to Father Karol. It said that Father Karol had to go to the big city of Warsaw. He had to leave right away. The Holy Father in Rome wanted to make Father Karol a bishop!

Bishop Karol was very busy. But he still had time to be with the children and young people. He was never too busy for them.

About nine years later, Bishop Karol received another message. Pope Paul VI wanted him to come to Rome. Pope Paul told Bishop Karol that he was very happy with his work. He made Bishop Karol a cardinal.

The Polish people were so very happy! When Cardinal Karol went back to Poland, the people had a big party for him.

Back to Rome

On August 6, 1978, Pope Paul VI died. He was a holy Pope. He had loved God and all people very much. Everyone was sad.

Cardinal Karol had to go to Rome again. All the cardinals had to go to Rome for an important meeting. The cardinals prayed. They asked God to help them choose another Pope.

The new Pope was John Paul I. He was very kind. He was always smiling.

Everyone loved the new Pope. He loved everyone, too. But Pope John Paul I was not feeling well. He was Pope for only thirty-three days. Then this good and kind Pope died.

All the cardinals and bishops were sad. All the people were sad. All the children were sad.

The cardinals went back to Rome. Cardinal Karol went, too. The cardinals met together. They talked and prayed. They were in a big room. The doors were all locked.

Many people waited outside. They waited for their new Pope to be chosen. They wanted to greet the new Holy Father. Who would he be?

The New Pope

On October 16, 1978, the people were looking at a chimney. The chimney was above the room where the cardinals were. At last the people saw white smoke! That was a signal. It meant that there was a new Pope!

The people clapped and sang. They cheered. They wanted to see their new Pope.

Soon a window opened. A cardinal came to the window and shouted, "We have a Pope! His name is Karol Wojtyla."

The people cheered and clapped again. Most of them had never heard of Cardinal Karol. But they knew that God had chosen him to be the new Pope.

The word "Pope" means "Father." The Pope is the leader of the Catholic Church. He is the father of people all over the world. The Pope is the Bishop of Rome today, just as St. Peter was the first Bishop of Rome. Every Pope takes the place of St. Peter and represents Jesus in a special way.

A Pope takes a new name. Cardinal Karol said, "My new name will be John Paul II."

John Paul II wants all people to be good and kind. He wants us to pray and go to Mass. He teaches us how to talk to God. He teaches us about God and his mother Mary. John Paul II loves children. He still says, "You are my favorites. The Pope loves you very much."

A Sad Day

One day something very sad happened. It was May 13, 1981. Pope John Paul was riding in the white "Popemobile" in St. Peter's Square, right outside the house where he lives.

Many people waved and clapped as he went by. Then, all of a sudden, someone shot him! Everyone was afraid that Pope John Paul would die. They prayed that God would make him better. They asked Mary to help him, because it was the anniversary of Mary's appearance at Fatima, Portugal.

The Pope was very sick for a long time. But God did make him well again. Did the Holy Father hate the man who shot him? No! He even went to visit him in prison. Pope John Paul told him, "You are my brother. Jesus loves you. I forgive you." That was a hard thing to say, but Jesus helped the Pope to say it. Jesus told us that we must love everyone—even people we don't like. Pope John Paul shows us how Jesus wants us to live.

The Great Missionary

Do you know what a missionary is? A missionary is a person who teaches other people about God. A missionary cares for the whole world.

Pope John Paul II is a great missionary. He wants to tell everyone about Jesus. Pope John Paul loves to pray. He prays every day for all people everywhere. He prays every day for peace in the world. He asks God to help us love one another. He shows us how to love one another.

Pope John Paul II travels all over the world. During his time as Pope, he has visited over 150 different countries! He has traveled over 700,000 miles! Did you know that that's like going to the moon and all the way back again *twice*?

Pope John Paul has come to the United States seven times and to Canada three times. He visits the poor and the rich. He visits the sick and people who are sad. In every country he asks the people to be fair and honest. He reminds them that Jesus wants them to treat others as they want to be treated. He says that the rich people must help the poor people. He tells people, "Jesus loves you!" This makes everyone so happy. They all say, "We love Jesus! We love you, too. You are our Holy Father!"

Many people also go to visit the Pope in Rome. He talks to them in their own language. Everyone can see him at his window. Sometimes he even walks or rides through the crowd. He blesses the grownups and children.

Full of Love

What will you remember about this story of Karol from Poland?

Maybe you will remember that Karol's heart is full of love for God and all people.

Maybe you will remember how far he has traveled to bring everyone God's love.

Maybe you will remember that as Pope John Paul II, Karol wants to tell every person in the world about God our Father and his wonderful love for us. He wants to tell everyone about Jesus, God's own Son, who came to earth to save us from our sins. The Pope wants to tell everyone about the Holy Spirit who gives us the love and help we need to live like Jesus. Pope John Paul knows that if we all try to live like Jesus, we can make the world a better place for everyone!

We are so happy that Pope John Paul is our Holy Father. We want to love and obey him. We want to help the Pope in his big job of leading the Catholic Church in the name of Jesus.

Let's pray for him every day!

Pauline
BOOKS & MEDIA

The Daughters of St. Paul operate book and media centers at the following addresses. Visit, call or write the one nearest you today, or find us on the World Wide Web, www.pauline.org

CALIFORNIA
3908 Sepulveda Blvd, Culver City,
 CA 90230   310-397-8676
5945 Balboa Avenue, San Diego,
 CA 92111   858-565-9181
46 Geary Street, San Francisco,
 CA 94108   415-781-5180

FLORIDA
145 S.W. 107th Avenue, Miami,
 FL 33174   305-559-6715

HAWAII
1143 Bishop Street, Honolulu,
 HI 96813   808-521-2731
 Neighbor Islands call: 800-259-8463

ILLINOIS
172 North Michigan Avenue,
 Chicago, IL 60601
 312-346-4228

LOUISIANA
4403 Veterans Memorial Blvd,
 Metairie, LA 70006
 504-887-7631

MASSACHUSETTS
885 Providence Hwy, Dedham,
 MA 02026   781-326-5385

MISSOURI
9804 Watson Road, St. Louis,
 MO 63126   314-965-3512

NEW JERSEY
561 U.S. Route 1, Wick Plaza, Edison,
 NJ 08817   732-572-1200

NEW YORK
150 East 52nd Street, New York,
 NY 10022   212-754-1110
78 Fort Place, Staten Island,
 NY 10301   718-447-5071

PENNSYLVANIA
9171-A Roosevelt Blvd, Philadelphia,
 PA 19114   215-676-9494

SOUTH CAROLINA
243 King Street, Charleston,
 SC 29401   843-577-0175

TENNESSEE
4811 Poplar Avenue, Memphis,
 TN 38117   901-761-2987

TEXAS
114 Main Plaza, San Antonio,
 TX 78205   210-224-8101

VIRGINIA
1025 King Street, Alexandria,
 VA 22314   703-549-3806

CANADA
3022 Dufferin Street, Toronto, Ontario,
 Canada M6B 3T5   416-781-9131
1155 Yonge Street, Toronto, Ontario,
 Canada M4T 1W2   416-934-3440

¡También somos su fuente para libros, videos y música en español!